LET'S BUILD A CUSTOM ORPHAN CARE STRATEGY FOR YOUR CHURCH

# LET'S BUILD A CUSTOM ORPHAN CARE STRATEGY FOR YOUR CHURCH

## AN INTERACTIVE WORKBOOK

## PATCH OUR PLANET

© 2020 by Patch Our Planet

All rights reserved. This book or any portion thereof may not be reproduced or used in any manner whatsoever without the express written permission of the publisher except for the use of brief quotations in a book review.

"Scripture quotations are from the ESV® Bible (The Holy Bible, English Standard Version®), copyright © 2001 by Crossway, a publishing ministry of Good News Publishers. Used by permission. All rights reserved."

ISBN: 978-1-7346919-1-7

# TABLE OF CONTENTS

Introduction/Invitation to Potential Team Members .................................................. 1
Let's Build a Custom Strategy for Your Church ...................................................... 3

## SESSION ONE: WHITEBOARD SESSION ............................................................ 5
    Team Members Assigned ................................................................................ 5
    Local Needs .................................................................................................. 7
    Global Needs ................................................................................................ 9
    Identify Gaps .............................................................................................. 10
    Identify Strengths ....................................................................................... 11
    Identify Ministry Momentum ...................................................................... 12
    Identify Potential Areas of Service .............................................................. 13
    Identify Past Ministries ............................................................................... 14
    Identify Your Most Critical Ministries ......................................................... 15
    Identify Your Dream Ministry ..................................................................... 16

## SESSION TWO: BUILD A LASTING FOUNDATION ............................................ 18
    Present-Year Timeline ................................................................................. 18
    Events by Month ........................................................................................ 19
    Two-to-Five-Year Plan ................................................................................ 21
    Six-to-Ten-Year Plan ................................................................................... 23

## SESSION THREE: ON-RAMPS FOR YOUR CHURCH TO GET INVOLVED ........... 25
    Entry Level ................................................................................................. 25
    Intermediate Level ..................................................................................... 27
    All-In Level ................................................................................................ 28

## SESSION FOUR: SUPPORT SYSTEMS ............................................................. 29

## SESSION FIVE: ESTABLISHING A CHURCH RESOURCE CENTER .................... 31

## SESSION SIX: ESTABLISHING FUNDS ........................................................... 33

## SESSION SEVEN: PREPARE FOR LAUNCH ..................................................... 35

## SESSION EIGHT: FINAL THOUGHTS .............................................................. 37

This book is dedicated to the amazing people who have faithfully supported Patch Our Planet over the years. This resource would not exist without you.

It is also dedicated to the passionate advocates who fight hard for the most vulnerable, the faithful church leaders who lead our local churches, and the precious children who dream of a forever family.

**LET THE CHURCH RISE.**

# INTRODUCTION

Every strategy should begin with prayer. We tend to make plans only by what our eyes can physically see or based on our experiences in life. But as a team, it is paramount to pay special attention to the direction the Lord wants your church to travel during this process. This may seem obvious. He knows the need already. But your position of humility and awareness to His leading will ensure the steps of your journey and protect the unity of your team. *Practical strategy* is in no way meant to convey a prayerless strategy. That would be a failing approach. We know the heart of God toward the orphan, so we should seek to represent that heart with a purposeful plan to stand up for those who need an advocate. If your team desires God's best, and it obviously does, then every team member should approach this process with humility and an openness to hear from the Lord.

This is not a process to finally get "our way" at church. It should be a process that humbly seeks God's heart and promotes unity within the church. With that in mind, you will find scripture encouragements throughout this workbook, hopefully a gentle reminder for you and your team to be anchored to God's Word and His Spirit throughout this process.

## SCRIPTURE ENCOURAGEMENT

*Commit your work to the Lord, and your plans will be established.*

—Proverbs 16:3

## INVITATION TO POTENTIAL TEAM MEMBERS

With the involvement of your church's leadership, invite three to seven trusted members to be a part of the process of building a custom orphan care strategy for your church. You may end up with three, or you may end up with seven. The number is not as important as placing *the right people* on the team. These are key people that will use their unique gifts to help craft a long-term orphan care strategy within a unified team setting. The goal of this process is to sift out the best way for your church to serve the orphan in your community and overseas. Be prepared for deep discussion. The following pages in this workbook will be a purposeful and practical guide to help your team more easily craft that long-term plan. Along the way, you will find a section on each page where team members can make notes during or between meetings.

## SCRIPTURE ENCOURAGEMENT

*May the God of endurance and encouragement grant you to live in such harmony with one another, in accord with Christ Jesus, that together you may with one voice glorify the God and Father of our Lord Jesus Christ.*

—Romans 15:5–6

## LET'S BUILD A CUSTOM STRATEGY FOR YOUR CHURCH

This workbook is a detailed guide to serve you during your team meetings. It will be an interactive process that will require honesty, vulnerability, and focused communication within your team. Depending on your meeting time constraints, this process should be broken up into several days. If you attempt to do this in one setting, brace yourself. It *can* be done. I like to refer to it as "digging through the weeds." But it can also be a deep and challenging effort. However, we are confident that the end result will bring a great victory for vulnerable children, broken families, your community, and your church. Don't forget that!

## DREAM FOR A MOMENT

Ask your team to share what their church orphan care ministry would look like if they were dreaming big. Invite them to share for a few minutes, and then ask if they are ready to start building toward that dream. Now let's get to work on making that dream a reality.

### STEP 1: DEFINE YOUR CHURCH'S MISSION

Let's begin by asking your team to summarize your church's local and global mission statements. Your team may have no idea, or it could be a simple statement that is well known throughout the entire church. If you are unsure, that's OK. It's time to find out. This first step is the beginning of a process that will build toward concrete solutions. It is the beginning of the sifting process that will ultimately lead your team toward a focused, intentional, and custom orphan care plan. Defining your church's mission will be like setting up an umbrella that will shelter your customized orphan care plan for the long haul. You want to make sure you are under it!

### LOCAL MISSION

_____

_____

_____

GLOBAL MISSION

_____
_____
_____

## SCRIPTURE ENCOURAGEMENT

*The steps of a man are established by the L*ORD*, when he delights in his way; though he fall, he shall not be cast headlong, for the L*ORD *upholds his hand.*

—Psalm 37:23–24

# SESSION ONE: WHITEBOARD SESSION

It is very important to have access to some type of whiteboard during your meetings so your team can actually see the ideas and make adjustments throughout the crafting phase. During this first whiteboard session, your team will be defining specific needs such as foster care needs in the community, the potential gaps in meeting those needs, strengths and momentum of your church's current ministry setup, and potential areas of local and global ministry. It will also shed light on past ministries, the most critical ministries, and your team's dream ministry.

Your team should spend time defining the major needs concerning foster care in the community. Your team may also be assigned the duty of defining the major needs of the orphans that your church is connected with globally. Knowing the needs will help your church work toward meeting those needs. It will also help your church leaders clearly explain to your church what the need is and how your church will help meet that need.

Note: Assign specific team members to capture and save the information off of the whiteboard or to take detailed notes throughout the process.

## TEAM MEMBERS ASSIGNED

_____

_____

_____

### SESSION INSIGHT

Remember, leaders' vision is usually about two years ahead of that of the people they are leading. That's OK! That just means that your team gets to be part of leading the effort to educate your church. Your team now needs to be the effective communicators from the front row. As a team, you identified the needs first. You helped craft the solutions. Now it will be your job to help educate and equip the church. In other words, don't get frustrated because everyone doesn't jump on board with your plan immediately. Team members that may not be used to running point on a project may need that encouraging reminder that they get to be a part of the process that helps change the DNA of the orphan care ministry at their church over time.

### SCRIPTURE ENCOURAGEMENT

*Open your mouth for the mute, for the rights of all who are destitute. Open your mouth, judge righteously, defend the rights of the poor and needy.*

—Proverbs 31:8–9

## LOCAL NEEDS

Locally, your team should start with the question, "How do we help get children into permanent, loving families and provide support?" Then your team should research your county statistics to get an idea of how many children are in foster care (and all relevant information, including children who age out and what organizations or churches are already working in the community). Your team should also take the broader perspective of thinking through how the current ministries of your church can actually be a part of the orphan care solution. For instance, your church may have an addiction recovery ministry that has had good success. Think of this ministry in terms of local orphan care. If your church can help hurting families find healing and help from addictions, you may be able to keep children out of the foster care system.

In addition, your church may have foster or adoptive families who feel isolated and unsupported. As your team thinks through the needs locally, make sure to take a broad, prayerful approach as to how to provide a solution. If our ultimate goal is to help children get into (or back into) loving families, then our churches should find ways to minister to broken families and provide opportunities for caring adults to become foster parents. Your church can then make it a priority to provide critical resources and wrap around these families on the front lines.

## LIST THE LOCAL NEEDS

_____

_____

_____

_____

_____

_____

_____

**NOTES**

**SCRIPTURE ENCOURAGEMENT**

*Whatever you do, work heartily, as for the Lord and not for men, knowing that from the Lord you will receive the inheritance as your reward. You are serving the Lord Christ.*

—Colossians 3:23–24

## GLOBAL NEEDS

Globally, your team should first ask the question, "How do we help get children into permanent, loving families and provide support?" The opportunity to help a child get into a forever family should override the need to experience all the emotions on a mission trip when you visit an orphanage. It is good and it is right to ask your team to take a deep, honest look at the progress of your global orphan care ministry (in light of the effectiveness of helping vulnerable children take the next step to find a forever family). Many churches discover throughout this process that many unintentional bad habits have been formed over the years. Now is the best time to make some of those crucial adjustments!

### LIST THE GLOBAL NEEDS

_____
_____
_____
_____
_____
_____
_____

## SCRIPTURE ENCOURAGEMENT

*How beautiful on the mountains are the feet of those who bring good news, who proclaim peace, who bring good tidings, who proclaim salvation, who say to Zion, "Your God reigns!"*
—Isaiah 52:7

### IDENTIFY GAPS

What's missing? Is there an obvious need that is going unmet? Recognizing gaps that may exist in the community will allow your church to see who is working where in your community (or globally). It will also help your team see how your church's strengths may be applied to fill that gap. Maybe your church has a vibrant volunteer base who would be great serving as mentors at a local boys' or girls' home. Or maybe your church has people who are already involved fostering or adopting who need support and resources from the church. It could be that your church has been doing what it has always done without looking into the actual impact of past ministries. This is the time for your team to begin to honestly discuss and identify the gaps that may exist.

### LIST THE GAPS

_____

_____

_____

_____

_____

_____

## SCRIPTURE ENCOURAGEMENT

*Bear one another's burdens, and so fulfill the law of Christ.*
—Galatians 6:2

## IDENTIFY STRENGTHS

Knowing the strengths of your church will allow your team to know where to start and where to focus their early energy. Orphan care ministry cannot be a sprint. It has to be a marathon. And the more "victories" your church experiences in the first year or two, the more volunteers you are likely to add because everyone loves being a part of a purposeful and effective ministry. That is the goal of this entire process. Everything should work toward a practical strategy that provides early *wins* with longevity for your team, your church, and certainly the children and families within your reach.

## LIST STRENGTHS

_____

_____

_____

_____

_____

_____

_____

## SCRIPTURE ENCOURAGEMENT

*The Lord is my strength and my shield; in him my heart trusts, and I am helped; my heart exults, and with my song I give thanks to him.*

—Psalm 28:7

### IDENTIFY MINISTRY MOMENTUM

Identifying ministry momentum can be advantageous because it will give your team a good understanding of where you will ultimately need to focus much of your attention during this building process. Is there an area in your orphan care ministry that your team can point to that has been especially impactful? Don't worry if your team is unable to unveil some of those areas. That just means there is a lot of untapped potential waiting to be developed!

### LIST AREAS OF MOMENTUM

_____

_____

_____

_____

_____

_____

## SCRIPTURE ENCOURAGEMENT

*I believe that I shall look upon the goodness of the Lord in the land of the living! Wait for the Lord; be strong, and let your heart take courage; wait for the Lord!*

—Psalm 27:13–14

## IDENTIFY POTENTIAL AREAS OF SERVICE

Have the team identify potential areas of service in the community. And if you are also working on a global strategy, begin to strategize the potential areas that may have been overlooked in your global partnerships. As the team begins to look at specific areas of service, try not to duplicate a ministry space that is being effectively filled by another church or organization. Instead, think of the gaps that were listed earlier, and then think of potential partnerships that your church could be a part of. That new partnership could add great momentum or bring new life to an existing ministry.

## LIST POTENTIAL AREAS OF SERVICE

_____
_____
_____
_____
_____
_____
_____

## SCRIPTURE ENCOURAGEMENT

*For God is not unjust so as to overlook your work and the love that you have shown for his name in serving the saints, as you still do.*

—Hebrews 6:10

### IDENTIFY PAST MINISTRIES

The goal for this section is for your team to honestly assess what orphan care ministry in your church has looked like in the past. Don't worry if you are in the ministry development stage. If you don't have a past ministry to pull from, then consider your journey a blank canvas of incredible potential.

### LIST PAST MINISTRIES

_____

_____

_____

_____

_____

_____

_____

## SCRIPTURE ENCOURAGEMENT

*Brothers, I do not consider that I have made it my own. But one thing I do: forgetting what lies behind and straining forward to what lies ahead, I press on toward the goal for the prize of the upward call of God in Christ Jesus.*
—Philippians 3:13–14

## IDENTIFY YOUR MOST CRITICAL MINISTRIES

As your team has taken an honest journey through this whiteboard process, there should be certain areas of ministry that rise to the surface above others. This session will allow your team to *focus on the absolute most critical ministry opportunities* in line with your church's mission. You may also find that some of your local and global funds are supporting ministries that don't align with your church's mission. That's OK. That's actually better than OK. This process should encourage and reward honest conversations as your team diligently seeks to focus on the most critical ministries. Far too often, churches take on too many ministry opportunities, equating busyness with effectiveness. Having too many disconnected or unfruitful ministries can easily tie your team's hands when it comes to making future announcements, asking for volunteers, or recruiting team members. Finding the most critical ministries will be like mining for a diamond. There can be a lot of dirt to work through before you discover something extraordinary—but it's worth it!

## LIST YOUR MOST CRITICAL MINISTRIES

_____

_____

_____

_____

_____

_____

_____

## SCRIPTURE ENCOURAGEMENT

*Let your eyes look directly forward, and your gaze be straight before you.*

—Proverbs 4:25

### IDENTIFY YOUR DREAM MINISTRY

Your team is present because each team member has, at one time or another, had a dream of making a big difference for vulnerable children. During this whiteboard process, your team should ask the question "What if?" What if resources and volunteers were never an issue? What would we do then? What if we could pull together a few other like-hearted churches in our community and begin a church orphan care network to share the great privilege of care? What if our global mind-set changed from building structures to building families?

There are dreams that need to be unearthed, those dreams that you began to discuss at the very beginning of this process. These dreams can become the basis for your six-to-ten-year vision plan for your church's orphan care ministry. Although your team will be focused on short-term victories during the early stages, every church should have a big dream that they are chasing. Ultimately, we all want the Church to be THE answer to the orphan crisis. Why not trust God and ask him to help you move those mountains?

### LIST YOUR TEAM'S DREAM MINISTRY (OR MINISTRIES)

_____

_____

_____

_____

_____

_____

_____

### SCRIPTURE ENCOURAGEMENT

*Delight yourself in the LORD, and he will give you the desires of your heart.*

—Psalm 37:4

# SESSION TWO: BUILD A LASTING FOUNDATION

A custom orphan care plan doesn't happen without lots of prayer and a concrete plan. Session Two pulls from the information that your team compiled during the whiteboard session. This is where your team begins to build a specific ministry plan that begins with achievable goals and grows with the vision over time.

The goal is to create an orphan care strategy that connects with 100 percent of the church, not just the people who are currently involved in it or most passionate about it.

Your team will put together a practical strategy, provide access to critical resources, learn effective communication, and implement the plan according to your final timeline. This is how you develop a lasting foundation, not one that fizzles during a pastor or staff change or one that diminishes over time if you lose your most passionate volunteer leaders. Your team should desire to put together a ministry plan that will outlast your team and your church leaders. You do this by making orphan care part of the DNA of the church. That means it is carefully crafted and intentional. Partnerships should be clear and well defined. The staff should understand the plan in simple terms. The church body should understand the clear on-ramps and opportunities of involvement. And your team should take advantage of the dedicated "orphan care" months (May and November) to highlight your ministry and provide opportunities of involvement.

## SESSION INSIGHT

Define roles of leadership at this point to help ensure implementation. Assign people in their areas of strength. No one wants to hear an off-key singer sing the national anthem. Likewise, no one wants to have a doctor who is nervous around people. Make sure your team gets people into the right places of service. By doing this, you will help them shine and bring benefit to the ministry in the most impactful ways. You want people to thrive in their areas of giftedness!

## SCRIPTURE ENCOURAGEMENT

*For no one can lay a foundation other than that which is laid, which is Jesus Christ.*
—1 Corinthians 3:11

### PRESENT-YEAR TIMELINE

These are specific actions to be taken in the first year (your team needs to define when the year begins and ends according to what time of year you are meeting). You will be using the list from the "Most Critical" whiteboard session to fill in this timeline.

Remember, you don't have to do it all in year one. Make sure that you build in enough space to prepare for each ministry event. Also, make sure you leave some margin afterward to celebrate and critique the ministry event. Our tendency is to do as much as possible in as little amount of time as possible. This is not an effective long-term strategy. Think about which ministry opportunities have risen to the top of that "Most Critical" list during the course of your whiteboard session with the team. Place only those top-tier critical ministry actions on the timeline below.

### LIST OF MOST CRITICAL MINISTRIES FOR PRESENT YEAR

_____

_____

_____

_____

_____

_____

_____

## SCRIPTURE ENCOURAGEMENT

*And let us not grow weary of doing good, for in due season we will reap, if we do not give up.*

—Galatians 6:9

## EVENTS BY MONTH

Now that your team has listed specific actions to be taken in the first year, you are ready to place those actions in a specific month. This step allows you to continue to break down the details of a yearly calendar. Remember that by focusing your events around those specific orphan care months (May/November), you have a better chance at echoing your ministry throughout the church because it will be planned in advance and a part of the church calendar/announcements.

Some advocates make the mistake of creating event after event, which inadvertently requires church leaders to make too many announcements. You can save them (and your ministry) from this stressor by creating a detailed calendar with margin and by communicating clearly with your church leaders before they put the church calendar together.

## LIST EVENTS BY MONTH

Jan.: _____

Feb.: _____

Mar.: _____

Apr.: _____

May: _____

June: _____

July: _____

Aug.: _____

Sept.: _____

## NOTES

Oct.: _____

Nov.: _____

Dec.: _____

### SCRIPTURE ENCOURAGEMENT

*Jesus looked at them and said, "With man it is impossible, but not with God. For all things are possible with God."*
—Mark 10:27

## TWO-TO-FIVE-YEAR PLAN

It is crucial to know where your ministry is heading after the first year. Obviously, there will be tweaks and adjustments along the way. But there must be a plan in place that will include those "second-tier" critical ministries that were too big for year one. Place those leftover critical ministries in the two-to-five-year plan, specifically in a year that makes the most sense for your church to pull it off with great enthusiasm.

## LIST YOUR LEFTOVER CRITICAL MINISTRIES

Second Year:

_____
_____
_____

Third Year:

_____
_____
_____

Fourth Year:

_____
_____
_____

# NOTES

Fifth Year:

_____

_____

_____

## SCRIPTURE ENCOURAGEMENT

*The heart of man plans his way, but the Lord establishes his steps.*
—Proverbs 16:9

## SIX-TO-TEN-YEAR PLAN

This section is where your team will list those ministry dreams that were captured earlier in the process. Your team will need to determine what year to place those dreams in. *Don't ever stop chasing those dreams!*

### LIST YOUR DREAM MINISTRIES

_____

_____

_____

_____

_____

_____

_____

### SESSION INSIGHT

Each year your orphan care team should gather together to review and renew the ten-year plan. As you move from year to year, you can use this same process to continue to develop and adjust the ministry as needed. Ultimately, your church should be setting up an orphan care ministry that plays to your church's strengths. Shave off those things that don't seem to have significant impact so your team can concentrate on what is most effective. Always include your church leaders in the process to avoid any misunderstandings or unmet expectations.

## SCRIPTURE ENCOURAGEMENT

*Where there is no prophetic vision the people cast off restraint, but blessed is he who keeps the law.*
—Proverbs 29:18

# SESSION THREE: ON-RAMPS FOR YOUR CHURCH TO GET INVOLVED

Think about this for a moment. If your team develops a ten-year plan, but the church leaders have no idea how to implement it or place volunteers, do you think you will find any real support or momentum? Probably not. That is why it is vital for a church staff to know where to put volunteers. There needs to be a pipeline. It is especially important that the church body knows how they can get involved. Identifying these on-ramps helps clarify the vision to the church while giving numerous ways for people to get involved according to their unique giftedness and callings upon their lives.

## ENTRY LEVEL

Your team determines what would be appropriate for the Entry Level. Think about ministry opportunities that most church members can be a part of (e.g., financial support, wraparound support, child sponsorship, event volunteers, encouraging social workers, visiting boys'/girls' homes, etc.). This opportunity should be communicated as 100 percent potential involvement from the pulpit and in Sunday schools, small groups, social media, and newsletters. Church-wide orphan care initiatives work great on special-emphasis dates (November: Orphan/Stand Sunday, National Adoption Month; May: Foster Care Awareness Month, Mother's Day; June: Father's Day).

## LIST ENTRY-LEVEL ON-RAMPS

_____

_____

_____

_____

## NOTES

_____

_____

_____

_____

### SCRIPTURE ENCOURAGEMENT

*Little children, let us not love in word or talk but in deed and in truth.*

—1 John 3:18

## INTERMEDIATE LEVEL

Expect less participation at this level than the Entry Level because of the greater commitment. Think of the top of the funnel being the Entry Level, with the widest appeal for participation. This second level would be the middle part of the funnel. Again, your team needs to define what an intermediate level of commitment will look like at your church. Here are some potential examples to help spark discussion for your team: short-term mission trips, Safe Families, guardian ad litem, mentoring a kid in a group home, respite provider, event coordinator, etc. Your team will likely come up with more of your own examples to be included.

### LIST INTERMEDIATE-LEVEL ON-RAMPS

_____
_____
_____
_____
_____
_____
_____
_____
_____
_____

## SCRIPTURE ENCOURAGEMENT

*I can do all things through him who strengthens me.*
—Philippians 4:13

### ALL-IN LEVEL

Internally, think of this level as the 5–10 percent, or the small end of the funnel. These are the front-liners. As your church leaders and your team share the need, you should never stop asking God to raise up people to help meet those needs. As your team discusses what the All-In Level looks like at your church, here are a few examples to start your conversation: foster care parent(s), adoptive parent(s), long-term mission to serve orphans, ministry leadership, etc. It should be a real priority for your church to make sure that volunteers at this level are especially equipped and prepared for their journeys. Early and on-going support for those on the front lines is one of the keys to a healthy long-term orphan care ministry and should be a main priority for your team.

### LIST ALL-IN LEVEL ON-RAMPS

_____

_____

_____

_____

_____

_____

_____

_____

_____

## SCRIPTURE ENCOURAGEMENT

*As each has received a gift, use it to serve one another, as good stewards of God's varied grace.*

—1 Peter 4:10

## SESSION FOUR: SUPPORT SYSTEMS

Support systems reach throughout the entire body of the church. A support system involves the whole church, while support groups tend to be smaller and made up of those in a similar situation. Support groups can be very beneficial in the overall healing process, but members of a support group can also become isolated in a crisis together. They need those far-reaching support systems throughout the entire body of the church.

*So what would orphan care support systems look like in your church?* It certainly begins in the most natural settings for close connections in your church, which may include small groups or Sunday school classes. Maybe it's a volunteer who commits to walking with a foster or adoptive family for a few months to make sure they are being equipped, encouraged, and supported during a major transition. Or maybe it's a volunteer who makes care packages for families to show them they are loved, prayed for, and thought about. It could be anything from a prayer team to a meal team or personal prayer cards for foster and adoptive families to share with their prayer network. Don't be afraid to be creative here.

Support systems spill outside the support-group room into the fabric of the broader church. Watch your people get behind the effort when they see their church providing practical solutions, serving vulnerable children, healing broken families, and wrapping around front-liners called to care. It's an opportunity for the church to share the hope of the gospel while representing God's heart for the orphan.

### SUPPORT SYSTEM IDEAS

_____

_____

_____

_____

_____

## NOTES

_____
_____
_____
_____
_____

**SCRIPTURE ENCOURAGEMENT**

*And let us consider how to stir up one another to love and good works…*

—Hebrews 10:24

# SESSION FIVE: ESTABLISHING A CHURCH RESOURCE CENTER

Foster and adoptive families will need all the help they can get before, during, and after care. By providing a resource center for your families, you are equipping them not only to survive but to thrive. In addition, you will also educate your church and potential future participants. It would be ideal to unveil your resource center at the same time you launch your foster care ministry.

## IDEAS

Provide video/book resources placed in a well-marked location in a library, coffee shop, or bookstore at your church. Also consider placing them on your church/ministry website (or create a separate one) for easy access online. Consider creating a care package of books, magazines, DVDs, videos, and other resources for foster/adoptive parents. Or turn those resources into specialized classes during regular church hours of operation where families can focus, connect, and learn while the kids are being cared for in childcare or small groups. Pay significant attention to special-needs support resources for families (behavioral challenges, counseling, trauma support, etc.). This may very well be the most challenging area for front-line families. At the same time, it's a great opportunity for the church to meet a tremendous need.

## BENEFITS OF RESOURCE CENTERS

Resource centers can help parents by reducing the costs associated with gaining helpful materials. It also lessens the financial burden on parents who are already spending a lot of money on their children. Resource centers may also encourage other church members to educate themselves and increase their interest in the church's orphan care vision.

## BEST OPTIONS FOR A RESOURCE CENTER AT YOUR CHURCH

_____
_____
_____
_____
_____
_____

### SCRIPTURE ENCOURAGEMENT

*And these words that I command you today shall be on your heart. You shall teach them diligently to your children, and shall talk of them when you sit in your house, and when you walk by the way, and when you lie down, and when you rise.*

—Deuteronomy 6:6–7

# SESSION SIX: ESTABLISHING FUNDS

## FOSTER CARE FUND

This fund is intended to assist foster families at your church with emergency needs. Try to avoid having able-bodied, trained families who are unable to take children due to the lack of beds, etc. Having an emergency fund like this will be an incredible blessing to those already-challenging life changes being experienced by family and child alike.

## GLOBAL ORPHAN FUND

The goal of this fund is to help with the expenses of indigenous adoptions through the church's global orphan partnerships. Is your church connected with another country? How could your church come alongside local churches in that country to help them care for the children in their community?

This fund can also be used to fund case managers and caregivers abroad to help bring accountability to the orphan work. Your church will find that your local ministry to children in foster care will likely accelerate your ability to serve and share with your global partnerships. A wise saying has been passed down over the years among advocates: "Local problems demand local solutions." What if your next global orphan care team not only raised support to travel but also raised money to help fund an adoption in that country?

## ADOPTION FUND

The purpose of this fund is to financially assist families in your church who are in the process of adoption either locally or globally. There are wonderful Christian organizations who will administrate and facilitate an adoption fund for your church, with your church's guidance, at minimal or no cost.

## NOTES

**WHICH FUNDS, IF ANY, DO WE WANT TO FOCUS ON FIRST?**

_____
_____
_____
_____
_____

### SCRIPTURE ENCOURAGEMENT

*You will be enriched in every way to be generous in every way, which through us will produce thanksgiving to God.*
—2 Corinthians 9:11

# SESSION SEVEN: PREPARE FOR LAUNCH

Clearly communicate the vision to the church by having a well-thought-out plan of communication. Show the church that your team is not only passionate about making a difference but prepared to the last detail. Your team's preparation will heighten trust and encourage involvement.

Your launch will be unique (and it should be). Below is one way we have seen churches unveil a new orphan care strategy during the worship service:

- Share a personal testimony (e.g., a former foster child, foster parents, your global team, a ministry partner in your community successfully working in that space, etc.).

- Give the biblical explanation of orphan care and the details of what your church will actually be doing to help provide a solution. Obviously, music and videos are great additions to clarify your vision and communicate effectively.

- Clarify your church's vision by distinguishing between what the vision used to be and what it will be. They need to hear how and why it is different—an honest assessment of the change.

- Connect your people by preparing bulletin inserts, response cards, engaging videos, and action points. Provide information and "next steps" at a central location the morning of the launch. Have your team ready and available to answer questions. Offer an informational meeting soon after launch, and incorporate an online strategy (e.g., church's resource website, a dedicated Facebook group, etc.).

## NOTES

**IDEAS FOR YOUR CHURCH'S LAUNCH**

_____
_____
_____
_____
_____
_____

### SCRIPTURE ENCOURAGEMENT

*The heart of the wise makes his speech judicious and adds persuasiveness to his lips.*

—Proverbs 16:3

# SESSION EIGHT: FINAL THOUGHTS

Invite your most organized team member(s) to assemble all of the team's ideas and put together the team's strategy and plan of communication into one document. It would be wise to gather again after this is done in order for each team member to hold a copy of the strategy, adjust any details, and then prayerfully move forward with accomplishing the strategy!

## LOCAL THOUGHTS

Your church's foster care ministry will be unique. It won't come together like someone else's. As your church leadership and foster care team prayerfully move forward, you can have great confidence knowing that God goes before the church that commits itself to taking care of the orphan. God has promised to illuminate our path. He's given us his lamp, the Bible, to light our path until the day when we no longer need the light: "And night will be no more. They will need no light of lamp or sun, for the Lord God will be their light, and they will reign forever and ever" (Rev. 22:5). But until that day, we will live out the gospel and take our responsibility seriously as we do our best to care for vulnerable children in our community.

## GLOBAL THOUGHTS

You can free your church to serve passionately around the world by creating a global orphan care framework that everyone can understand. Your church leaders should understand it. The people in your church should understand it. Then you can focus on training your global teams to do the most long-term good on behalf of every orphan. Many orphanage directors around the world are hanging on by a thread. They need the local church to step up. They need the local church to rally to the cry of the orphan. Instead of focusing on what your church can accomplish in the short term, please think of how you can help your global partners get children into loving forever families in the long term. Every child needs a family and deserves our best effort.

### FINAL THOUGHTS

Don't let past procedures dictate how you minister in the future. Allow God to illuminate your hearts and minds with what he wants to accomplish through your team. In the end, it's going to take all of us. The problem is too large to take on by ourselves. Your church can be the inspiration for other churches. Your step may be just the step needed to inspire other churches to join hands in a church network of care, where each church has their own strategy but meets together to pray and share best practices with each other. It is in this way that churches in a community can share the great privilege of care. May God's heart for orphans exponentially grow in your church, and may he grant you wisdom and unity along the way.

### SCRIPTURE ENCOURAGEMENT

*Religion that is pure and undefiled before God the Father is this: to visit orphans and widows in their affliction, and to keep oneself unstained from the world.*

—James 1:27

**PATCHOURPLANET.ORG**

www.ingramcontent.com/pod-product-compliance
Lightning Source LLC
Chambersburg PA
CBHW061358090426

42743CB00002B/61